MW01114884

DIPLOMATS IN THE TRENCHES

PROFILES OF U.S. FOREIGN SERVICE OFFICERS

NICHOLAS KRALEV

Also by Nicholas Kralev:

America's Other Army: The U.S. Foreign Service and 21st-Century Diplomacy

Decoding Air Travel: A Guide to Saving on Airfare and Flying in Luxury

Copyright © 2016 by Nicholas Kralev

Editors: Darrell Delamaide and Markus Nottelmann
Consultant: Barbara Slavin
Cover design by Jennifer Fleischmann

ISBN-10: 1535421401
ISBN-13: 978-1535421409

Published October 2016

Contents

Foreword

Most Americans, like ordinary people everywhere, don't relate to diplomacy—to the extent they think about it at all, they view it as something that happens in a stratosphere of officialdom, far out of their reach. They also believe that it has little to do with their lives.

I reached this conclusion after more than a decade of research focused on the practice, impact and perceptions of diplomacy in the 21st century, conducted in dozens of countries. My second conclusion, having to do with reality, is markedly different from the first, which is about perception. Despite the oddity and impracticality of the diplomatic protocol, etiquette and grandstanding, the substance of diplomacy does have a direct impact on the lives of real people.

By "real people" I mean all of us, as we go about our business and deal with normal everyday things, hoping for the safety and well-being that can help us lead a decent life and fulfill our potential.

We live in a globalized and interconnected world, and whether we realize it or not, we are affected by events, forces, trends and people far beyond our national borders. What happens in other countries, and how our diplomats deal with it, has an impact on our security, prosperity, health, privacy, ability to travel and much more. If they keep dangerous foreign citizens out of our country, negotiate trade agreements that create jobs at home, succeed in containing and eradicating deadly outbreaks, and persuade other governments to crack down on human trafficking, we can all sleep better and enjoy our way of life. Failure, on the other hand, can threaten that way of life.

Average Americans may not relate to diplomacy, but they do relate to other people's stories—and diplomats have incredible stories to tell. While few dine with kings and queens, many more are targeted by terrorists, carjacked or exposed to severe pollution and epidemic diseases.

A natural successor to *America's Other Army*, which focused on the U.S. Foreign Service as an institution, this book is about some of its members—about their work and their lives, because diplomacy is not just a profession. It affects every aspect of a diplomat's life, and that of his or her family.

The Foreign Service has about 13,000 members, some 8,000 of whom are officers, or diplomats. So there are many more than the ones included in these pages whose stories deserve to be told—and perhaps they will be, in future volumes of this work. It's all up to the readers.

Matthew Ference

Improvising in a
'Non-Permissive Environment'

Matthew Ference belongs to a select group of American diplomats who passed the Foreign Service entrance exams on their first try. He attributes it to being relaxed and trying not to care too much.

When he applied in 2003, Ference, whose most recent assignment is as the public affairs officer at the U.S. Embassy in Laos, had already been accepted to two graduate programs. So he "didn't study for the exams or expect to pass, which reduced the pressure immeasurably," he said. "I didn't grow up dreaming of being a diplomat, so I approached the written and oral exams like any other test—great if I passed, but not the end of the world if I failed."

Photo by U.S. Mission Laos

More than 20,000 Americans apply to join the Foreign Service every year, but only several hundred are hired, depending on budget constraints and the service's needs. About 40 percent of all candidates pass the written exam on average each time it is offered, according to the State Department, though many take it more than once. It's a standardized multiple-choice test with questions about history, politics, economics, geography, popular culture and other areas, and also includes an essay. It doesn't test for knowledge of the history or functions of diplomacy.

Of those who make it to the oral assessment, about a third are successful on average. It consists of a group exercise based on a case study of a fictitious country where the U.S. Embassy must deal with a certain situation, as well as an individual interview and a case-management exercise, in which each candidate must write a memo to a superior recommending a course of action.

State Department officials said they look for "basic skills" and the "broadest applicant pool," noting that "there is no one path or group of experiences that will lead you to the Foreign Service." Dozens of professions are represented in the service, including some that have little or nothing to do with international affairs, such as neuroscience, urban planning and the food industry. Since 9/11, the number of former members of the military has increased significantly.

A former U.S. Army infantryman, Ference didn't deploy to a war zone during his military service—he did, however, as a diplomat. In 2010, he was assigned as a political reporting officer on a so-called provincial reconstruction team in the Iraqi city of Karbala. More than 30 such civil-military teams were created about a decade ago to help stabilize and rebuild the war-torn country amid a ruthless insurgency. Three of them—in Kirkuk, Erbil and Basra—became U.S. consulates after the U.S. military withdrawal at the end of 2011. The rest were disbanded.

Most provincial reconstruction teams were housed by military bases and used trailers as living quarters, and sometimes even as offices. While the bases in major cities like Mosul had a few thousand American troops, in Karbala there were only about 100, Ference said. The base there was the only U.S. facility in the province. He shared an office trailer with five other team members, while his living trailer was divided into three rooms, each about 8 feet by 8 feet. "The bathroom trailer, with showers, was about a 50-foot walk," he said. "We had a gym, a cafeteria, a basketball court with a broken rim, and a volleyball court. The ground was gravel and dirt, and became very muddy when it rained."

Service in war zones, and particularly on provincial reconstruction teams, became known as expeditionary diplomacy. The Foreign Service wasn't prepared to work in such conditions, so its learning curve was steep and improvising was essential. Diplomats aren't armed, but those going to high-danger posts were given a "two-hour orientation to firearms," Ference said, in case they needed to use a weapon for self-protection. Once on the ground, "we had to improvise" in what was known as a "non-permissive environment," and "hope that the Foreign Service selection process brings in people who have versatility and adaptability," he added.

After Karbala, Ference was the public affairs officer in Erbil, the capital of the autonomous Kurdistan Region in northern Iraq, and helped transition the provincial reconstruction team there to a consulate. When I visited in 2012, he hosted a program about democracy and federalism in Iraq for political science students from the University of Kurdistan. The speaker was an Iraqi Ph.D. candidate and son of a prominent Islamist political leader.

"We invite people to the American Cultural Center, so we can stimulate discussion on politics, society and culture," said Ference, who has also served in Thailand and South Korea. "We've had talks about language, the environment, music and other subjects. It's a place where Americans and Iraqis can get together and share their views on different topics, where we can learn from each other. Even if I'm the only American in the room, it's often the first time our audience has ever had the chance to talk to a U.S. government official."

Ference noticed a big difference when he arrived in Erbil from Karbala. "I think the basic reason that Erbil is different from the rest of our

Photo by U.S. Mission Laos

posts in Iraq is that the population of Iraqi Kurdistan and its govern-ment truly want us to be here," he said. "The positive developments in the Kurdistan Region after the 1991 Gulf war, and again after 2003, have happened under the umbrella of U.S. protection, and people here are eager for continued and deeper engagement. If anything, they want more U.S. presence, rather than less. That is not the case in the rest of Iraq, where feelings are mixed."

Ference and a colleague took me to visit a school built with U.S. as-sistance, which paid for half of the $1.6 million project. "It became one of the most popular schools in the region, and I met lots of parents in-terested in sending their children there," Ference said. "We also used the school to host other educational programs, including teaching dis-advantaged and vulnerable women English and computer skills, so they could find jobs in Erbil's booming economy."

The Mar Qardakh School, where many of the students from kinder-garten through grade 12 were Christians, but other religious groups were welcome as well, was more modern than some U.S. schools.

"A true picture of the work done in Iraq would recognize that there have been both successes and failures," Ference said.

Virginia Blaser

Getting 'Beaten Up'
for 'Doing Things Right'

Virginia Blaser, a newly minted American diplomat, was the duty officer at the U.S. Embassy in Madrid one weekend in 1993 when a
call came in from two Midwest teachers who had brought a group of
teenage students to Spain on their first trip abroad.

A boy from the group was nowhere to be found, and the teachers
wanted the embassy's help to locate him before word about his disap-
pearance reached his parents back home. Blaser alerted the police but
couldn't just sit and wait for something to happen.

"I remember thinking that the child might be out there hurt or
scared," she recalled. "So my husband and I literally walked the streets

Photo by U.S. Mission Tanzania

for two days, hoping that we'd find him just by sheer luck, but of course we didn't. Eventually, we got a call from the police saying that they had been driving along a highway outside the city and found him—traumatized, dehydrated and sunburned."

Now a senior Foreign Service officer and deputy chief of mission in Tanzania, Blaser has also served in Uganda, Mauritius, El Salvador, Britain and Belgium, while managing to raise four children. She started out as a consular officer, eager to help fellow Americans abroad. "It may not be a big deal for you when you see hundreds of people a year, but it is a big deal for a little lady from Des Moines who has never traveled overseas and has had her bags grabbed and has been pushed around," Blaser said. "I love to be the one who can solve her problems."

While assisting Americans overseas was cited by dozens of officers serving around the world as the best part of consular work, they had few good things to say about interviewing applicants for U.S. entry visas. "Even if you say 'no' nicely, some people still yell at you and try to spit on you," Blaser said. "It took me weeks not to take that personally, because I'd never had anyone speak to me that way before. Sometimes, they even threaten your life."

Consular officers don't always want to receive feedback from their customers, but Blaser did hope to hear back about the lost boy in Madrid during her first tour in the service. While she was looking for him, his parents and their congressman's and senator's offices had been calling several times a day.

When the boy arrived at the embassy, Blaser took him home against official rules, phoned his parents, fed him, gave him clothes and a bed for the night. "Finally, the next day, the group leader came to pick him up," she said. "We gave him another set of clothes, they left and we never heard from anyone again—not from the parents, not from the senator or congressman, not from the school. I suppose in a way that was a compliment, if everybody was satisfied and had no complaints. I don't usually feel that we need thanks for doing our job. But it was one of the few times I actually wanted someone to call and say that the kid was all right." No one returned the clothes, either.

Blaser did hear back from two Colorado women she had helped in London in the spring of 2003—but only through the media. The women, whose rental car had been broken into and their purses stolen with their passports and money, called on a Friday morning to ask for help. A local British employee at the embassy explained to them the procedure for applying for temporary passports so they could return home, telling them they needed to submit photos and pay a fee. They arrived at the embassy, with their luggage, a few minutes before it was to close. Visitors are usually not allowed in the building with more than a small bag or purse for security reasons, but the guards saw the women were frustrated and let them bring the suitcases into the lobby of the American Citizens Services section.

Even though the embassy was closing for the week and most of Blaser's staff were preparing to go home, she asked for volunteers to work overtime so they could start processing the women's passport applications.

"This wasn't a true emergency, because they weren't leaving the country until Monday, and there was time to do everything that morning, but because they were so upset and angry, I wanted to do as much as we could that night," Blaser said. One local employee was recovering from cancer and needed rest, yet she offered to stay. Another one did, too, although his father had just had a heart attack that afternoon and the son was expected at the hospital, as Blaser learned three days later. Most of the paperwork was done, and the only thing left before the passports could be issued was mandatory name checks, which could take hours. Since her staff had already put in an extra hour, Blaser requested the name checks and asked the women to return first thing Monday morning to receive their passports. They did and made their flight back home later that day.

A couple of weeks passed, and one day an article appeared in the Denver Post. The two women, high school teachers Jennifer Tompkins and Irma Sturgell, had told columnist Diane Carman their story—it was about the "hell" they had endured with the "nightmare embassy staff."

Photo by U.S. Mission Uganda

Blaser's heart sank as soon as she glanced at the headline: "Travelers see Brits' best, Yanks' worst."

"The embassy staff was unconscionably rude. The women didn't have the money and the photos required to get new passports, the bureaucrats said. They refused to allow them to make any calls," Carman wrote in the column, which has since been removed from the newspaper's website. "We were still pleading, but they physically took our suitcases and put them on the street," she quoted one of the women as saying. "They said if we had been beaten or raped, they could help us. That would have been considered an emergency. It was unbelievably inhumane."

Both Blaser and the embassy spokesman at the time, Lee McClenny, said that Carman hadn't contacted them to ask for their version of the story. Carman confirmed that in a 2004 e-mail message but offered no explanation why not. The column reinforced the perception about callous bureaucrats at embassies who care more about obeying rules and going home on time than helping people in need. Members of Congress often hear such complaints from constituents. Except that this time was different.

"That was such a small case, and there have been thousands since then," Blaser said, "but it still bothers me, because it was my staff that made sacrifices and did everything right, only to get beaten up in that article."

Michael Hammer

'You Can't Learn Diplomacy Through Osmosis'

Michael Hammer was nine years into his Foreign Service career in 1997, when he did advance work on President Bill Clinton's visit to Vancouver, Canada, for the annual Asia-Pacific Economic Cooperation summit.

Hammer with Ricky Martin. Photo by U.S. Mission Chile

Once the president's party arrived, Glyn Davies, a fellow Foreign Service officer who was the executive secretary of the National Security Council (NSC) at the time, approached Hammer with a special task. Clinton wanted to go out to dinner with a group of friends, and Davies wondered if Hammer, who had been in the city for about 10 days, could help.

Even though Hammer was a mid-level political officer, he had no problem making a dinner reservation. "I had in essence a 30-minute bus ride to make arrangements, but I did manage to find a restaurant close by, and everybody ended up having a good evening out," he recalled.

About a year later, when it was time to bid on available positions for his next assignment, Hammer was interested in a job in the NSC's Europe office and sent his résumé to Davies. "Glyn came back and said, 'I don't necessarily see a match for the Europe job, but there is a vacancy in our press shop at the NSC.' I was pretty stunned," Hammer said.

That job changed his career. It got him started in press work, and eventually led to his appointment as the first NSC spokesman in the Obama White House, and later as assistant secretary of state for public affairs. From there, he became ambassador to Chile in 2014. He said he doesn't believe any of that would have happened had he not arranged that dinner for Clinton in Vancouver.

"If someone comes to you, and you are able to do little things right, you might be given bigger opportunities," he said. "People don't necessarily focus on whether you are the best note-taker or cable-writer, but if you have a good head on your shoulders, and you can solve problems, then perhaps you'll be given other opportunities."

Personal connections and corridor reputation play a significant role in selecting candidates from the Foreign Service bid lists for rotating positions at embassies, consulates and multilateral missions, as well as in Washington—perhaps more significant than some diplomats deem appropriate. Still, managers are generally unlikely to hire someone just because they know him or her, without proper qualifications. Since joining the service in 1988, Hammer has also served in Bolivia, Norway, Iceland and Denmark.

Few professions have changed as much as diplomacy has as a result of the 9/11 attacks. The shift has been so big that diplomats have had to acquire skills and perform duties that were never expected of them before, and were not even associated with diplomacy, including working in active war zones. "That challenged our identity," Hammer said. "We knew what we came in to do, but all of a sudden we were asked to do something different."

The wars in Iraq and Afghanistan, in particular, were "a shock to the system," he said. "We hadn't worked in war zones and done things like infrastructure and local governance, which we hadn't come in trained and expected to do. You have to go back to the Vietnam generation to find people who did things like that, and it wasn't quite the same. But now, if we have to do nation-building again or pass certain skills on to foreign governments, we know how to do it."

The public caught an unprecedented glimpse of the behind-the-scenes workings of U.S. diplomacy through an unauthorized release of more than 250,000 State Department cables—some of them secret—by the website WikiLeaks in 2010. The documents, written by American diplomats posted across the world, provided information and analysis on developments in other countries, foreign officials and U.S. embassy activities.

"Such reckless sharing of classified information jeopardizes our relationships and puts sources, such as human rights activists, in harm's way," Hammer said. "There is always an expectation that they talk to us in confidence. Diplomacy does need that space behind closed doors to take effect and produce results. People will be more willing to talk to you and do things for you if they are allowed that breathing space."

At the same time, the cables made a surprising revelation to the public. "People suddenly realized three things," Hammer said. "First, that we are pretty good writers and provide sound and interesting analysis. Second, that we are passionate and determined to advance the U.S. national interest. Third, that we do what we say, and there isn't much variance between what we say in private and in public."

Photo by U.S. Mission Chile

Serving their country is by far the most cited reason for joining the Foreign Service by American diplomats, though a desire to travel and see the world, as well as financial security, are often mentioned as well. "First and foremost, we are patriots," Hammer said. "We come in because we want to serve the country. We want to advance American interests. What we don't necessarily know when we come in is how we are going to do that."

Even with all the publicly available information on the State Department website, existing literature and the many blogs of serving diplomats that have appeared in recent years, new Foreign Service officers don't know exactly what to expect. What they do depends on their specific future assignments in a highly unpredictable career path.

Despite recent improvements in training, following decades of neglect, many new officers still arrive at their first post without sufficient knowledge about the specifics of what an embassy and its various sections do, several senior officers said. The State Department culture still doesn't value training and professional development at different levels as highly as it should, and relies too heavily on diplomats' ability to figure things out on the job, they added.

Hammer said the ever-increasing demands of modern diplomacy, along with the new skill sets required to achieve the Foreign Service's ambitious mission, make high-quality training more urgent than ever.

"Diplomacy in the 21st century has so many dimensions that you can't just learn it on your own or through osmosis," he said.

Yuri Kim

'Diplomacy Isn't Always About Being Nice to People'

Yuri Kim never thought this would happen. It was a cold February day in 2008, and she was sitting in North Korea's largest concert hall, listening to a performance by the New York Philharmonic—not far from where she was born in South Korea.

A political officer in the Foreign Service, Kim had no apparent reason to be accompanying the renowned American orchestra to the world's most isolated country, which would have been more suitable for a public diplomacy officer. But it was precisely her task on that unprecedented trip.

Yuri Kim in Baghdad. Photo courtesy of Yuri Kim

She was an aide to Christopher Hill, the assistant secretary of state for East Asian and Pacific affairs at the time, who was leading high-stakes talks with Pyongyang aimed at dismantling its nuclear weapons program. The concert tour was a "carrot," which Washington hoped—though it didn't admit publicly—would improve the North's cooperation in the tough talks. Kim had actually negotiated the visit with the com-munist government, traveling to Pyongyang on two previous occasions with the philharmonic's leadership.

"They didn't want to send Chris, because that would have been too high level, so they sent me," she said. "I helped develop the program and negotiate the terms of the visit."

A naturalized American who moved from South Korea to Guam when she was 3, Kim joined the Foreign Service in 1996, during a pe-riod of pitiful resources for diplomacy and minimal hiring of new offi-cers. She chose to go to Beijing on her first tour, followed by Tokyo. Then she returned to Washington for a stint on "the line"—a State De-partment term for the group of mid-level officers staffing the secretary of state and advancing his or her travels. At the time, the top U.S. diplo-mat was Colin Powell. "He would walk into a room or hotel lobby, and people would spontaneously get up and start applauding," Kim said. "They didn't do it for the president, the vice president or anybody else I could see."

After that assignment, Kim went to Seoul. During her tour as chief of the embassy's internal political unit, she met dozens of political and business leaders, journalists and academics. One of those acquain-tances was a vice president at Asiana Airlines, South Korea's second-largest carrier. A couple of years later, that connection would pay off big time.

Kim and the members of the New York Philharmonic had just flown to Beijing on a commercial flight from the United States, on their way to Pyongyang for the 2008 concert tour. But it turned out there was no plane big enough to take the entire party to North Korea. So Kim called her Asiana contact, and a Boeing 747 was promptly dispatched from Seoul—free of charge. "It was a big PR coup for Asiana," she said.

Having spent the first dozen years of her Foreign Service career in Asia and Washington, and having learned Chinese and Japanese, in ad-dition to her native Korean, Kim decided it was time to gain some expe-rience in another region. "I knew that Iraq would continue to reverber-ate for a long time" in U.S. foreign policy, she said, and many of her col-leagues had already volunteered to serve there since Saddam Hussein's 2003 overthrow, "so it was my turn."

At the time, career diplomats serving in Iraq were allowed so-called linked assignments in any country of their choice after completing their war-zone tours. Not surprisingly, many chose London, Paris, Berlin or other plush posts. But Kim passed on the link and went to Turkey, as the political counselor at the embassy in Ankara. "I didn't want Iraq to be a one-off" assignment in that region, she said. "I wanted it to be the foundation of something more substantive. Turkey was emerging as a significant regional power, and I thought service there would be meaningful."

Throughout her career, Kim added, she has tried to "work on exciting issues that people care about and that have an impact," and to build a diverse skill set, including "achieving operational objectives, learning how to negotiate, managing people and running an embassy."

For decades, diplomacy was an almost exclusive club of mostly white male elites who dealt with foreign countries' elites, mainly their governments. That is no longer the case. The Foreign Service is still very selective, because it naturally wants the most qualified candidates—to quote Kim, "We aspire to be elite, though not elitist." But today any U.S. citizen between the ages of 21 and 60 who passes written and oral exams can become a diplomat, even without a college degree. While the service still has a long way to go, now it looks more and more like America —in terms of ethnicity, gender, religion, educational and professional background, and even country of birth.

Kim advised Foreign Service applicants to think hard about whether the diplomatic lifestyle is for them—living abroad for extended periods of time while moving to a different country every two or three years. In addition, it may be difficult for female officers in particular to find a partner if they join the service single. "I think it's harder for women to find someone who is willing to pick up, leave his life behind and follow you around the world," she said. Ultimately, both single and married

Photo courtesy of Yuri Kim

officers make sacrifices, she added, pointing out the challenges of rais-ing a family on the go, and away from relatives and friends back home.

Kim, who became chief of staff to Deputy Secretary of State Antony Blinken in 2015, questioned the widely accepted meaning of the word "diplomatic" as nice and tactful.

"It's not always about being nice to people or not saying hurtful things. In fact, in the jobs that I've had to do, we've had difficult and sometimes combative conversations," she said. "In the most acute cases, like North Korea or Iraq, it's about talking to someone so that guns don't get pulled out. It's a way to avoid or end conflict, and to get people to compromise."

Gavin Sundwall

'Any American, Any Problem, Any Time'

Gavin Sundwall stood beside the grave, a Bible in hand, and read John 11:25-26: "I am the resurrection and the life..." Two taxi drivers, who had become the deceased woman's chauffeurs during the last years of her life, shared memories of her and shed tears. They sprinkled the woman's ashes over the graves of her two husbands, which were just a few feet apart.

The impromptu ceremony at the Corozal American Cemetery outside Panama City in the summer of 1998 was over. Sundwall, a first-tour Foreign Service officer, had never met the elderly American woman when she was alive, even though she had lived in Panama for decades. He saw her for the first time when he went to the morgue to identify her body after she had died from natural causes. That was no unusual duty for him as a consular officer, but the funeral he organized was certainly not in his job description.

Photo courtesy of Gavin Sundwall

"I informed her family back in the U.S. of her death, but they didn't want to come down and have anything to do with her burial, although they sent money," Sundwall recalled. "They told us that her last wishes had been to be cremated and have her ashes sprinkled over the graves of her two husbands. All her friends were elderly and didn't want to come. So who else would have done it if I hadn't?"

That same year marked the first time Sundwall was in a Panamanian jail. Two Satanist killers sat across from him. Fortunately for him, he was just visiting the criminals, who were U.S. citizens, to make sure they were being treated humanely, and to relay any messages to their families back home.

Later during that tour, Sundwall received a call one day from an Indiana couple who had just adopted a girl from Panama and wanted to take the baby to her new home in the United States. But the airline they flew on refused to allow the infant on the plane. She didn't have a U.S. entry visa, and though she was now the daughter of American citizens, she was still a national of Panama.

As it turned out, the couple "had done all the adoption paperwork through the Panamanian system, but had done nothing on the American side," Sundwall said. "She was an abandoned and burned girl who had been put in a trash can and set on fire. The [adoptive] parents had scheduled hospital treatment for her the next week and had appointments for reconstructive surgery. So it was very hard, but I had to sit them down and tell them that there was nothing I could do to help them out of this situation that day, since the Immigration and Naturalization Service declined to allow them to enter the U.S. without a visa under humanitarian parole. It was one of the hardest things I've had to do in my career."

Sundwall explained to the new parents that they had to go back home and apply for adoption, which includes visits by social workers to determine whether they would be capable parents. Then, they had to file an application for an immigrant visa for the girl, which would make her a permanent U.S. resident, and later an American citizen.

"At the end of the day, they had to put the child back into the orphanage, go back to the United States and start the process. I told them they could call me anytime to talk about anything they wanted," Sundwall said. But the process dragged on, and the couple got frustrated with the immigration authorities who seemed to come up with hurdle after hurdle. At Sundwall's suggestion, the couple took the matter to the office of their U.S. senator, Richard Lugar. "They were back in my office within a month after that first time, and we issued the visa," Sundwall said.

According to the State Department, the United States "welcomes more children through adoption than any other nation"—almost a quarter-million since 1999. In 1994, the Bureau of Consular Affairs created the Office the Chidren's Issues, which assists "parents as they seek to provide a home to orphans abroad through inter-country adoption by offering country-specific information about the adoption process, and by advocating for greater protections for adoptive parents and children abroad."

Sundwall's stories from Panama may seem extreme and not quite representative of daily consular work, but they are actually very common. Almost every consular officer has similar life-changing stories, and they certainly don't always end happily.

There was no happy ending—at least not yet—to the story of a 24-year-old U.S. graduate student who went missing while hiking alone in southern China in 2004. Sundwall was chief of the American Citizens Services section at the embassy in Beijing, having served in Kuwait after leaving Panama. The student, David Sneddon, was a Mormon missionary from Utah traveling through China at the end of his study there when he vanished in the Tiger Leaping Gorge. His family flew to China and, with the help of the embassy, recreated his last steps and met with senior local officials. The U.S. ambassador at the time, Clark Randt, raised the issue at the highest levels of the central government in Beijing. Robert Bennett, a Republican U.S. senator from Utah at the time, also got involved.

Although the family didn't find Sneddon or his remains, it was "very grateful for the full cooperation and support" of both the embassy and the State Department. "The ambassador was most gracious, considerate

Gavin Sundwall in Kabul. Photo courtesy of Gavin Sundwall

and interested in our situation," the student's parents wrote on a website created to help find David. "The embassy and staff of American Citizens Services have gone beyond the 'second mile' in their continuing efforts to help."

Sundwall, who later changed his career track from consular to public diplomacy, has also served in the Azores, Afghanistan and Denmark, where he became the public affairs officer at the embassy in Copenhagen in 2014. He has many other stories about Americans abroad to tell. There was the elderly Chinese-American woman who got lost in Beijing with $3,000 in her pocket. Then there was the American man and his Chinese wife who were being blackmailed by their landlord. And of course, there are suicides, traffic accidents and other fatalities, as well as passports and visas for new American spouses and children.

In China, together with one entry-level Foreign Service officer and three local Chinese employees, Sundwall covered a consular district larger than Western Europe—and, as he pointed out, "it's much harder to do business in China than in Western Europe." While there are "limitations on what we can do and how much we can get involved," Sundwall said, "our job is really any American, any problem, any time."

Official U.S. policy is not to take sides in child-custody disputes, but at the same time consular officers have a duty to protect U.S. citizens. That apparent contradiction makes these cases even more difficult. Officers protect the interests of the American parent and child by negotiating—they actually try to avoid using that word—on their behalf with local authorities and sometimes with the other parent.

Sundwall exhausted all his persuasive skills over three days in the fall of 2002 in a hotel room in central China, where Camille Colvin and her 4-year-old son Griffin were held by police at the request of the boy's Chinese father, Guo Rui. He had kidnapped his son from New York, after a U.S. divorce court had awarded custody to his ex-wife. She had hired a detective and found Griffin in Guo's hometown of Zhengzhou but wasn't allowed to leave the country—or even the hotel—unless she left the child behind or reached an agreement with Guo.

"She was besieged," recalled Sundwall, who flew down from Beijing to handle the case. "The Chinese said it would have to go through the Chinese court system, which was going to take a while, and she agreed, but there was a lot of pressure on her to make one of those informal deals to settle things with the father. At one point, I was trying to persuade the Chinese to let me take the child to my house in Beijing not to be trapped in that hotel."

In the end, Colvin had to pay $60,000 in "blood money," Sundwall said, even though she won custody in a Chinese court.

Anjalina Sen

Wearing Flip-Flops
More Often Than Suits

Anjalina Sen is a diplomat of a peculiar kind. She finds diplomatic receptions "a bit more onerous than sleeping in a bamboo hut for a week." It makes sense, then, that she has spent her nine years in the Foreign Service so far working mostly on refugee issues.

"We do a lot of business at receptions, but the field work I do is phenomenal," she said. "Talking to refugees about their experience, their hopes and dreams, and figuring out how to bring that up with our policy—that's what gets me really excited. I'm often in refugee camps, so I spend a lot of time in flip flops. I don't like wearing a suit."

Photo courtesy of Anjalina Sen

Born to a Canadian mother and an Indian father, Sen grew up in Brazil, Mexico and Portugal. After working on Wall Street, she made what seemed a natural career choice for someone with her cosmopolitan upbringing.

Soon after joining the Foreign Service, she found herself in the middle of the now-infamous passport crisis of 2007, when new entry requirements for Americans traveling to Canada and other countries in the Western Hemisphere caused a huge flood of passport applications, overwhelming the State Department. In a very unusual move, Sen and most of her entry-level colleagues were assigned to an emergency task force to help ease the load.

"We didn't have enough computers and had to hand-adjudicate passport applications," she said. "But it was a great bonding experience, and I'm still really close with the people I was on that task force with."

After her mandatory consular tour, which she spent in Guangzhou, China, Sen became a refugee officer in Bangkok. That was the start of a career path that is highly unusual even in an already unusual organization like the Foreign Service. While most officers try to take a variety of assignments over the course of their careers, Sen has stayed true to refugee work ever since, helping to protect refugees across Asia and the Middle East, and to resettle some of them in the United States.

"I see my job as translating cultures and negotiating to find similarities," she said. "We do a lot of monitoring and evaluation. The U.S. is usually the largest donor in the camps I visit, so we fund nutrition, medical services, preventative and curative healthcare, water and sanitation, gender-based anti-violence and other programs. We don't get out and tell the story very much. We do humanitarian work, but we don't benefit from it necessarily."

In addition to the humanitarian reasons, Washington spends significant resources to help refugees—regardless of whether they end up in the United States—out of concern that large camps full of desperate people with no prospects and decent living conditions could ignite violence and cause regional instability.

According to the U.N. High Commissioner for Refugees (UNHCR), there were more than 65 million forcibly displaced people worldwide in 2015. Among them were more than 21 million refugees, over half of whom were under the age of 18. That same year, U.S. government shows that the United States admitted nearly 70,000 refugees, most of whom were from Burma and Iraq. Washington was criticized for accepting only 1,682 Syrians in 2015.

Sen said the process of designating displaced people as refugees and resettling them is rather long. "We have several bars to meet before we can even consider sending them to the U.S.," she explained. "UNHCR has the international mandate, and individuals enter the process as persons of concern. Then they become asylum-seekers, go through refugee status determination, and then get the refugee designation. However, that doesn't mean they are refugees under U.S. law quite yet—for that to happen, UNHCR has to formally refer a person for resettlement, and then the Department of Homeland Security has to make a decision on admissibility to the United States."

Throughout that lengthy and uncertain process, those displaced people need protection and assistance, and that's where Sen and her colleagues come in. "We are in a situation where no one is willing to speak for these people but us," she said. After Thailand, she was posted to Iraq, followed by a public diplomacy assignment in Colombia. But she missed refugee work and left Bogota early, eventually returning to Iraq and then heading to Lebanon. She will be dealing with refugees again for the next three years in Turkey, beginning later this summer.

As hierarchical as a government bureaucracy is, Sen sees significant change for the better in the Foreign Service—especially in her line of work—compared to other countries' diplomatic institutions. "I have family in the Indian Foreign Service, and it's so hierarchical," she said. "When I look at my counterparts, it's very much about your rank. Here, it's about getting the work done, and I feel empowered."

For a long time, Sen was concerned that her personal life might suffer because of her work. She was in a long-term relationship when she joined the Foreign Service, but during her first tour in China, her boyfriend was able to come only as a tourist on short-term visas.

Photo courtesy of Anjalina Sen

Employment was out of the question. "We had different ideas about what we wanted our lives to look like," and the relationship ended, she said. "Many of us join the service as double-income families, but then all of a sudden we drop to a single income—and it's often the lower income," said Sen, who was single for about six years until 2015, when she met someone else.

"In most cases, we have partners who are just as educated and motivated, and we are asking them to sit out on their career for lengthy periods of time," she said. "That aspect of Foreign Service life is very difficult."

David Lindwall

From 'Observing and Reporting' to 'Advocacy and Lobbying'

Working saved David Lindwall's life—literally. He was deputy chief of mission at the U.S. Embassy in Haiti in January 2010, when a catastrophic earthquake flattened his house. He felt very lucky to be in the quake-resistant embassy building when the earth shook.

His colleague Victoria DeLong, however, wasn't that lucky—she was killed when her house collapsed. Hundreds of thousands of people and a quarter-million buildings perished. DeLong, who was the embassy's cultural affairs officer, spent 27 of her 57 years in the Foreign Service.

David Lindwall in Haiti after the 2010 earthquake.
Photo courtesy of David Lindwall

For American diplomats serving abroad, natural disasters, along with terrorist attacks, carjackings, kidnappings, robberies and even murder, are part of their way of life. Yet many, including Lindwall, are drawn to dangerous postings more often than plush ones. After Haiti, the poorest country in the Western Hemisphere, Lindwall went to Iraq. He cut short his next assignment as consul-general in Guayaquil, Ecuador, to serve in Afghanistan. In 2016, he finally made it to the first world, when he became deputy chief of mission in Sweden.

"Even though not every officer has had such experiences, dealing with disasters is very much a part of the Foreign Service life," Lindwall said. "After my house in Haiti collapsed, I slept with the Marines that first night. The second night, the Marines brought a cod, a pillow and a blanket into my office. I slept there for about six weeks."

Lindwall, who joined the Foreign Service in 1985, has also served in Colombia, Spain, Honduras, Nicaragua and Paraguay. He said the most significant change in what American diplomats do during his time in the service has been a shift from observing and reporting to advocacy and lobbying.

"We used to lobby the executive branch, but that's not enough any-more," he said. "In many countries, the center of power is not only in the central government, and we have to deal with a much broader field of players, such as legislatures, mayors, governors and even the private sector. We have to build constituencies."

Beginning in the 1990s, the embassy in Guatemala tried for more than a decade to persuade the Central American country to reform its child-adoption system. Rampant corruption was hampering many Americans' attempts to adopt Guatemalan children. From 1999 to 2013, U.S. citizens adopted more children from Guatemala—almost 30,000— than from any other country except China and Russia.

The corruption "created a situation where babies were being stolen" without the future American parents' knowledge, said Lindwall, who was deputy chief of mission there in the mid-2000s. Congress put "an incredible amount of pressure" on the embassy to push for changing the system, he said. "Guatemala was a historic violator of human rights, but on that we didn't get nearly the pressure that we did on adoption."

Lindwall and his colleagues mounted an intensive lobbying cam-paign among Guatemalan legislators, government officials and others involved in the issue—and finally succeeded.

While the executive branch of the U.S. government usually sets the country's diplomatic agenda—and overseas missions often have flexibil-ity in the daily management of foreign relations—the field has become more competitive. Congress plays a major role in foreign policy through legislation, foreign travel and appropriating funds. In addition, the Sen-ate must confirm every ambassador, as well as assistant secretaries and higher-ranking officials at the State Department.

During his time as the political-military counselor at the embassy in Baghdad, beginning in 2011, Lindwall was involved in another campaign driven largely by congressional pressure.

Camp Ashraf was a refugee camp in Iraq that looked nothing like the camps familiar to Americans from the news. Rather, it resembled a small town, with modern buildings, the latest communications technology and even its own university, Lindwall said. When he first visited, he was impressed by a "huge mosque with a monumental blue dome, a museum, water park, several monuments, a large conference center, and a tree-lined main boulevard."

The camp was the headquarters of the People's Mujahedin of Iran, which is also known as Mojahedin-e Khalq or MEK, an Iranian resistance group designated by the State Department as a foreign terrorist organization "for the assassination of several U.S. military personnel and civilians in the 1970s." Following the 2003 U.S. occupation of Iraq, the American military disarmed the camp, which had about 3,400 residents, according to the department. The new Iraqi government was under pressure from Tehran to close Ashraf for years, but the MEK refused to leave. The Iraqi army attacked the camp more than once, killing several Iranians and provoking an outrage in Congress.

So it fell on the United States to help find a new home for the refugees and to close Ashraf. A direct link between Ashraf's future and the U.S. national interest was difficult to find, but it was the issue that occupied more of Lindwall's time in Iraq than any other, and the "U.S. government spent an incredible amount of time and resources on it."

Photo by U.S. Mission Haiti

He explained that paradox with "an effective lobbying campaign that a few vocal MEK supporters" mounted in Washington. "Somehow, they persuaded 98 members of Congress to sign a letter" to then-Secretary of State Hillary Clinton, calling for the group's removal from the terrorist blacklist. "These were very serious people," Lindwall said of the legislators, "so there was a great deal of pressure on us to resolve this problem."

In 2012, hundreds of Ashraf residents moved to a former U.S. military base near the Baghdad airport, Camp Hurriya. By 2015, most of the rest had been relocated as well.

Among the most lucrative and controversial trades the United States does around the world are the sales of weapons and other military equipment, which are overseen and authorized by the State Department. When authorizing deals, the department said it takes into account the overall situation in the purchasing country, including its human rights record, potential weapons proliferation and regional security.

Officers like Lindwall "do the screening and paperwork," he said, though the Pentagon "originates the deals." That was another part of his work in Iraq. Since Saddam Hussein's demise in 2003, the government there has made U.S. arms purchases worth more than $20 billion, including dozens of F-16 aircraft.

"They ultimately want to have an air force to match their neighbors' who have hundreds of planes apiece," Lindwall said. "That creates a lot of jobs in the U.S."

Victoria Nuland

'Diplomacy Is About People to People'

Victoria Nuland wasn't necessarily looking for love when she joined the Foreign Service in 1984, but she found it anyway—fairly quickly and not too far away. While working on the China desk at the State Department, she started dating a young speechwriter for then-Secretary of State George Shultz.

When they got married three years later, the inevitable question arose: What would her husband, Robert Kagan, do while his diplomat-wife served abroad? He didn't think that joining the Foreign Service himself would be the best solution, and he really wanted to write. So that was what he did.

"He wrote his first book, on Nicaragua, in the spare bedroom of our Moscow apartment," recalled Nuland, who was a political officer at the U.S. Embassy in Russia from 1991 until 1993. "The KGB used to rifle his office regularly—we could tell by the lingering stench of cigarettes and body odor. They couldn't fathom that he was really just a writer."

Photo by U.S. Mission Germany

Since then, Nuland has built a career that is the envy of many American diplomats. She was the first female ambassador to NATO, beginning in 1999, and became assistant secretary of state for European and Eurasian affairs in 2013—most of her colleagues never get to be ambassadors, let alone assistant secretaries.

But she is most proud of having achieved a balance of sorts between her work and personal life—raising a family and keeping a spouse happy. She attributed it to "lots of luck, great mentors and a heavy dose of bending the Foreign Service to be more modern" and accommodating. "I married a very flexible, portable guy who was willing to make huge sacrifices in his own career to make mine possible, and who had generous bosses," she said.

After more than three decades in the Foreign Service, Nuland said that today's global challenges require American diplomats to be "agents of change" and to effectively get specific things done in multicultural environments, working not only with governments, but also with NGOs, the private sector and even individual citizens in foreign countries.

"Diplomacy is not only about government to government anymore, but also human to human," she said. "What we try to do, and get other countries to do, is empower people. American diplomacy is increasingly done from the bottom up. We recognize that, with the craving for democracy and freedom of expression, with the Internet and social media, countries are changing as much from the bottom up as they are from the top down. So we need to know those people and be connected to them."

For decades, U.S. diplomats in the Middle East were used to "working with kings, sultans and presidents for life," Nuland said. "But they didn't know much about the people in those countries. They didn't know how to promote democracy or manage economic support funds. Then we had the revolutions in Tunisia, Libya, Egypt and Syria. So those officers have had to change and learn new skills, because we need transformational folks."

Nuland has been criticized for being too much of an activist in pushing for stronger support for Ukraine's pro-democracy movement and standing up to Russian activities in the former Soviet republic. Washington's frustrations with the more hesitant and indecisive European Union were laid bare in a leaked 2014 phone conversation between Nuland and the U.S. ambassador in Kiev, Geoffrey Pyatt, in which she disparaged the EU, using a well-known four-letter word. U.S. officials suggested that the call had been bugged by the Russians.

Despite the embarrassment that episode caused, Nuland didn't lose the confidence of her bosses. In fact, she has enjoyed the trust and support of the country's top political leaders from both parties for decades and has been rewarded with senior positions by both Republicans and Democrats.

During the George W. Bush administration, she was an adviser to Vice President Dick Cheney. During President Obama's first term, then-Secretary of State Hillary Clinton's decision to appoint her the State Department spokesperson surprised many, but Nuland had been valued by Democrats before—in the Clinton administration, she was chief of staff to Deputy Secretary of State Strobe Talbott. When John Kerry succeeded Clinton in 2013, he put Nuland in charge of the Bureau of European and Eurasian affairs.

So how can the same person champion the policies of Bush and Cheney, and a few years later do the same with Obama, Clinton and Kerry's policies? "My fundamental starting point is that everybody in these top jobs, whether Cheney or Clinton, has a single common thread, which is that they love their country, and fundamentally what they want is to do what's best for America," Nuland said. "Then you have to be willing to politely challenge assumptions that you think are wrong. However, once you've made your case, and if they choose to move forward in a different direction, your job is to implement what they chose to do, or to say that you can't and you'd like to be somewhere else."

When the Bush administration launched a unilateral attack on Taliban-ruled Afghanistan shortly after 9/11, Nuland was deputy chief of the U.S. Mission to NATO in Brussels. She and her boss, Ambassador Nicholas Burns, thought that getting other countries to join the U.S. operation would bring long-term benefits in the global fight against terrorism. But the powers in Washington weren't interested.

Photo by U.S. Mission Georgia

"We spent four or five months saying to the White House, 'We get it, you don't want allies at the front of the spear, but they can help hold the spear, and here's how.' They ignored us, ignored us, ignored us, and then finally started saying, 'All right, we'll do some of this.' We felt that we opened their eyes to the possibility of getting the allies on board," Nuland recalled. Eventually, dozens of countries joined the international forces in Afghanistan.

While Nuland was climbing the Foreign Service ladder, her husband wasn't doing too badly, either. During that first NATO assignment, Kagan followed her to Brussels, where he helped to take care of their two children and began writing another book. That book, "Of Paradise and Power," was his first bestseller and established him as a leading thinker and writer on foreign affairs. "He reminded me that he wrote it as a direct result of coming to Europe with me," Nuland said. "More broadly, he credits Foreign Service spousehood with deepening his global education."

The State Department has become more flexible and accommodating in recent years when it comes to the needs of Foreign Service families, she noted. "In 1998, when I asked for my second maternity leave in 18 months, the Human Resources folks looked at me like I had two heads—and then said yes," she said. "Now it's routine for mothers and fathers to be granted generous leave without pay or telecommuting options for each kid, or if a parent or partner needs them."

Although Kagan, who is a senior fellow at the Brookings Institution, has given up a lot to follow her overseas, Nuland said she has had to make some sacrifices, too. "I've spent two-thirds of my career in Washington to accommodate Bob and the kids, including turning down the first two ambassadorships I was offered in the late 1990s, because they didn't work for the family," she said. Her children wanted to attend high school in the United States, so during those years she took herself "out of the ambassadorial sweepstakes again, including for some very interesting posts," she added.

"I love the job—it's all I've ever wanted to do—but I love my husband and kids more," Nuland said. "We've always made all our decisions together."

Brian A. Nichols

'We Need to Groom' Minority Diplomats for Senior Positions

Brian A. Nichols was a 24-year-old newcomer to the Foreign Service in the fall of 1989, when he arrived in Peru for his first overseas posting. Over the next few years, terrorist attacks, including on U.S. diplomatic facilities, were frequent occurrences in the South American country. It was peaceful and much changed when he returned as ambassador in 2014, but he says his house remains the most attacked ambassador's residence in the world.

The terrorism threats and other security challenges that marked Nichols' first tour provided a preview of what was to come in an increasingly dangerous diplomatic career. After Peru, he served in El Salvador at the end of the Central American country's civil war. During his

Photo by U.S. Mission Peru

assignment as political counselor in Indonesia, which began weeks before 9/11, extremists linked to al-Qaeda killed 202 people, including seven Americans, at a nightclub in Bali. Less than a year later, a suicide bomber murdered a dozen people at the JW Marriott hotel in Jakarta.

Nichols said he and his colleagues at the embassy warned the Indonesian government about potential terrorist activities in the country with the world's largest Muslim population soon after 9/11. However, "we didn't get much of a response," he recalled. "There was a lot of resistance, because most Indonesians were dismissive that al-Qaeda-led terrorism existed in their country. The overwhelming sentiment was that Indonesian Islam is tolerant, which was certainly true, but there was some extremism—there were groups willing to use violence to achieve their goals."

The main such group was Jemaah Islamiyah, which was responsible for the Bali bombing. After that massacre, the Indonesian government "finally understood the gravity of the problem and could no longer ignore our requests" to start building counter-terrorism capabilities, Nichols said. "They realized that this type of violent extremism was a threat to religious harmony, and they made a mental shift to deal with the problem from a law-enforcement standpoint."

The embassy worked to "give them the tools" to investigate and prosecute those responsible for terrorist attacks, and to establish a police anti-terrorism unit, Nichols said. "We also worked with members of religious organizations, the media, universities and others to get popular support for dealing with the threat of extremism and terror," he added. "Australia was a major partner in this effort, as were other Western governments."

Good diplomats understand cultural specificities and sensitivities in the countries where they serve, and Nichols learned something new about Indonesians during a police press conference to announce the capture of the perpetrators of the Bali bombing, who were there in handcuffs. "They were smiling and laughing," Nichols said. "We wondered why they were so jovial. Our local counterparts told us that's what Indonesians do when they are guilty. So that left no doubt about the suspects' guilt in the minds of the public."

Jemaah Islamiyah was significantly weakened at the time, with its leaders and hundreds of followers behind bars. However, reports began appearing in 2015 that the group was active again, fundraising, recruiting, and even sending members to train in Syria.

Nichols continued to deal with terror-related issues as deputy chief of mission in Colombia, beginning in 2007, including the added dimension of narcoterrorism. The government's decades-long armed conflict with the militant movement FARC brought death, destruction and fear into the lives of all Colombians, along with efforts by American diplomats, military and intelligence officers to help end the de facto war.

In 2008, Nichols and his embassy colleagues were involved in a successful attempt to rescue 15 hostages, including three American contractors, who had been kidnapped by FARC rebels more than five years earlier. While that was a Colombian operation, "we were able to provide intelligence and technical support," Nichols said. "It was incredibly satisfying to see these Americans free after all those years."

In August 2016, Colombian President Juan Manuel Santos announced that, after four years of negotiations, his government had reached a peace deal with the FARC. The conflict is estimated to have claimed more than 200,000 lives.

Not all of Nichols' work in the Foreign Service has been dangerous and depressing. As principal deputy assistant secretary for international narcotics and law-enforcement affairs at the State Department before he returned to Peru as ambassador, he oversaw various efforts in Afghanistan and Pakistan. He said he was especially proud of programs that gave "women and girls access to justice," including education and training in the United States and their own countries, which "changed their lives."

Nichols and his wife, Geraldine Kam, have two girls of their own. They were toddlers at the time of the Bali bombing, and their mother left Indonesia with them for over six months as part of an embassy evacuation of dependents. That was the only time when the family was apart. Both Nichols and Kam were in the Foreign Service when they met in 1994, and when they got married, they decided that they their "key goal was not to be separated and to raise the children together."

Nichols and his wife, Geraldine Kam. Photo by U.S. Mission Peru

Nichols said that his wife has made more career sacrifices than he has. She could be in a senior position at another embassy, but she chose to take unpaid leave and go to Peru as a spouse—nepotism rules don't allow her to work for her ambassador-husband.

As a black and an Asian-American officer, respectively, Nichols and Kam represent small minorities in the Foreign Service—black officers are only 5 percent, and Asian-Americans are 7 percent. Susan Rice, President Barack Obama's national security adviser, criticized the lack of diversity among America's diplomats and the rest of the foreign policy workforce in a May 2016 speech. "In the halls of power, in the faces of our national security leaders, America is still not truly reflected," she said.

Nichols said that, until the early 2000s, the State Department "didn't recruit for diversity aggressively enough." In recent years, the department has said that it wants a Foreign Service that "looks more like America," but "these policies will take time to play out," Nichols said.

"We are competing with Wall Street, Silicon Valley, academia and other places where talented people go. For couples, both members expect to work and have fulfilling careers, and that's still a challenge for us. I'd like to see more resources for recruitment, as well retention and salaries," he said. "We also need to make sure that we groom and select a more diverse group of career people to serve in deputy chief of mission, ambassador and deputy assistant secretary positions, because they prepare us to be assistant secretaries and undersecretaries."

Sumreen Mirza

When Your Workplace
Is a Terror Target

Sumreen Mirza's path to the Foreign Service began in her parents' homeland, Pakistan. She was an intern at an NGO in the southern port city of Karachi in 2002, when the U.S. Consulate there was attacked in a massive explosion that killed 12 Pakistanis.

Mirza's proximity to the terrorist act and the torn-down consulate wall had an unexpected effect: instead of scaring her, it made her consider a diplomatic career. "I thought I could make a difference on the other side of that wall," she recalled. "I had a background in urban planning and environmental engineering, and worked for the Army Corps of Engineers." That background determined Mirza's choice of management and administration work as her career track in the Foreign Service when she joined in 2005. Her first posting was as a management officer at the consulate in another Pakistani city, Peshawar.

Photo by U.S. Mission China

"One of my big challenges was to find new land and space for operations," she said. "We were in a very small building, and we were very close to a major street and intersection, so it was easy for a car bomber to attack us—and a couple of years after I left, that's exactly what happened."

That 2010 assault, which included a truck bomb, machine guns and rocket launchers, killed six Pakistanis and wounded 20. As in Karachi, there were no American casualties. The attackers failed to breach the outer perimeter of the compound but demolished part of an exterior wall. In early 2016, two Pakistani employees of the consulate were killed by an explosive device while on a drug-eradication mission.

Mirza became one of several general services officers at the U.S. Embassy in Beijing in 2014. Between her first and present assignments, she worked at the State Department in Washington, and dabbled in two other "cones," to use Foreign Service jargon—she did her mandatory consular tour in Paris and served as a political reporting officer in Iraq.

At the embassy in Baghdad, where I first met her in 2012, Mirza covered the Kurdish political parties. Although there was an American consulate in the Kurdistan region in northern Iraq that did its own reporting, her job was "to understand the Kurds' role in national politics," she explained. "The Kurdish Alliance has almost 60 seats in the parliament, and they have been a mediator in political crises, as well as a kingmaker in the political formation. I meet with them almost every day—in the parliament, the ministries, in NGOs."

While much of diplomatic work has changed in recent years, requiring new skills to address current challenges, reporting and analysis are still essential in what embassies and consulates do. Hundreds of cables are sent to Washington every day, and their authors often wonder if anyone reads them. Senior officials at the State Department insisted that they are read widely, including at other agencies. In fact, they added, when WikiLeaks published more than 250,000 cables—some of them secret—in 2010, the department had to tighten other agencies' access to its system, because the person who leaked the documents was from another agency.

"The WikiLeaks episode has changed a bit of our writing. We are more careful about protecting sources and other people," Mirza said. In Baghdad, she wrote "almost every day—cables, meeting notes, spot reports or other messages." A political tradecraft course she took at the Foreign Service Institute before moving to Iraq "gives you the basic tools, and then you come here and pick up the style and template that suits the management, the interlocutors and the conversations we have," she said.

Mirza experienced a luxury of sorts in Baghdad: a weeklong overlap with her predecessor in the same position. The State Department has struggled for decades to address the problem of staffing gaps—usually in the summer—when incumbents depart at the end of their tours weeks before their successors arrive. In the past, personnel shortfalls made overlaps nearly impossible. Now the Foreign Service is much larger, but there is another problem: parents want to leave after their children's school year has ended, and to arrive at their new post just before the new school year begins—with some home leave and possibly training in between.

The bid list with available Foreign Service positions is one of the most anticipated internal documents the State Department puts out, along with the promotion list. It comes out twice a year—once for the main summer rotation cycle, and a shorter version for the winter cycle. Then it's updated periodically, as positions are added or removed. The importance of the bid list and the lobbying that takes place over the following months cannot be overstated. Every three years, or less for hardship posts, U.S. diplomats have to decide where in the world they should go next—which position might offer a rewarding experience and possibly a promotion, but also which post might meet the needs of the entire family.

So it's hardly surprising that Foreign Service members take this career-shaping and potentially life-changing process very seriously. Yet many of them don't fully understand it. Who exactly decides who goes where? Can Human Resources overrule the post's choice? Is the direct supervisor of the future employee the one who has the biggest say? What if he or she is rotating out and won't actually supervise the incoming officer?

Photo courtesy of Sumreen Mirza

The question that puzzles most officers is this: On what criteria are decisions based? There is no clear answer, and the process is opaque and subjective, hundreds of officers said. Some decision-makers prefer previous experience in the respective region, they said, while others would rather take someone who has performed superbly in another region. Some like—or at least don't mind—being "lobbied" by bidding officers, while others hate that. Some value "corridor reputation," while others care little for it. These uncertainties are particularly hard on officers in the early part of their careers, Mirza said.

"I don't have a solution, so I have a hard time criticizing the process, but it's just opaque, because lobbying happens on all levels and in different places," she said. "You must be qualified for the job, but who you know, and who they know, also matters."

Hans Wechsel

Finding Your Own Way
to Make a Difference

Hans Wechsel was a 29-year-old restaurant manager in Oregon with a degree in secondary education in 1999, when his career took a drastic turn. Having passed the Foreign Service entrance exams despite his lack of foreign affairs experience, he became a diplomat.

"What a great system for someone like me, where you can, based on merit and ability, get into a career like this," said Wechsel, whose résumé at the time also included seasonal work as a tour guide at Yellowstone National Park. His first assignment in the service was in the West African country of Ghana.

New career diplomats often wonder how long it will take them to be entrusted with truly important work and make a real difference. Many of their senior colleagues say they will have a chance to prove themselves in the first five years. Since 9/11, the opportunities for entry-level officers to take on significant responsibilities have increased, allowing them to manage people and large budgets.

Photo by Leslie Wechsel

Wechsel ended up making a crucial difference during his second tour, as a political officer at the U.S. Embassy in Brussels, where he was responsible for the counterterrorism portfolio and had frequent interactions with various parts of the Belgian judicial system. In 2003, he came upon an unusual law, about which the United States had little reason to worry until then.

"Belgium came up with the idea that, for certain crimes against humanity, regardless of where they took place and who committed them, Belgium had the obligation and competence to pursue a case," he said. "It's commonly referred to as 'universal jurisdiction.' That concept was mixed with the idea that any citizen could bring a criminal complaint, and force at least a cursory investigation."

Shortly before the Iraq war started, victims of a Baghdad bombing during the first Gulf War in 1991 filed a war-crimes complaint against top U.S. officials at that time, including President George H. W. Bush, Defense Secretary Dick Cheney and Colin Powell, who was then chairman of the Joint Chiefs of Staff. At the time of the complaint, Cheney was vice president and Powell was secretary of state in the George W. Bush administration.

Although arrests couldn't be made just on the basis of a complaint, Wechsel explained, "at a certain point during an investigation, a judge could decide that there was enough evidence to make an arrest, but they wouldn't make an announcement, so how do you know? While arrests were hugely remote possibilities, there was no absolute guarantee that they wouldn't happen" if the named officials went to Belgium, which hosts both the EU and NATO headquarters, Wechsel said.

Before the story appeared in the media, he got the attention of his superiors at the embassy and in Washington, who decided on a dual course of action. First, get the complaint, and any others that might be filed, dismissed. Second, repeal the law.

The diplomatic work paid off. By the time the press focused on the issue, a parliamentary committee had introduced changes to the law to allow the government to block such cases. The long-term solution, however, took several months, during which Washington threatened to seek moving the NATO headquarters to another country to avoid visits to Belgium by affected U.S. officials. Powell called the law a "serious problem." It was repealed in August 2003, following some not very pleasant public exchanges between the U.S. and Belgian authorities.

Even as a junior officer, Wechsel played an important role. "Both my government and the Belgian government recognized me as an expert on the issue, and I was in meetings with the Belgian prime minister," he said. "I had contacts with different perspectives and agendas. I knew the lawyer for the NGO that was helping file those complaints, as well as the member of parliament who had authored the law. I had contacts in the Justice and Foreign Ministries, and also had a working relationship with the federal prosecutor. So I had the whole circle—everybody who had a major stake."

Wechsel faced a very different challenge when he arrived at his next post in Abu Dhabi in 2004. He was the first regional director for the Arabian Peninsula of the Middle East Partnership Initiative (MEPI), which the Bush administration had created two years earlier to help build and strengthen civil society, and to support the region's democratic aspirations.

Wechsel's main task was to find local organizations in eight countries — Bahrain, Jordan, Kuwait, Oman, Qatar, Saudi Arabia, Yemen and the United Arab Emirates—and award them grants for projects promoting the U.S. agenda. "The way a society is governed is important to whether extremism develops or not," he said. "So we try to get to the roots of terrorism by addressing not only political rights, but also economic opportunity, education, women's rights, because these are all linked."

In 2005, a 26-year-old Yemeni woman, Tawakkul Karman, co-founded a group called Women Journalists Without Chains to promote human rights and press freedom. With great ambitions but almost no funds, Karman wasn't able to make a big difference at the beginning—until Wechsel and his team met her and gave her organization a grant for a pilot project to seek freedoms, rights and protections for journalists in non-democratic Yemen. "I don't want to overstate the case, but we did launch her as an activist with capacity," Wechsel said. "Eventually, her impact became greater, and she has never looked back."

Photo by Leslie Wechsel

Karman went on to became the public face of Yemen's 2011 uprising as part of the Arab Spring pro-democracy movement, with massive protests against the rule of then-President Ali Abdullah Saleh, who had been in power longer than Karman had been alive. She was even called "the mother of the revolution."

That same year, the 32-year-old mother of three became the first Arab woman to receive the Nobel Peace Prize, which she shared with two Liberian women, President Ellen Johnson Sirleaf and peace activist Leymah Gbowee. "In the most trying circumstances, both before and during the Arab Spring, Tawakkul Karman has played a leading part in the struggle for women's rights and for democracy and peace in Yemen," the Nobel Committee said at the time.

A few years after Wechsel left Abu Dhabi, the MEPI office was closed under pressure from the UAE government. He later served as one of several "Iran watchers" stationed in countries with ties to the Islamic Republic, in his case Turkey—the United States has no diplomatic relations with Iran, and consequently no physical presence there. Wechsel said he made contacts with Iranian asylum-seekers, as well as "people who still live in Iran but travel to Turkey, and Turks who visit Iran or maintain connections there." He also met with Iranian opposition leaders, journalists, academics, student activists and human rights lawyers.

Iran and North Korea are the only countries with which the United States has no diplomatic ties. Washington's engagement with the rest of the world is extraordinarily deep and broad. The sheer number of issues being worked on at any given time makes the U.S. Foreign Service the closest thing there is to a global diplomatic service. In fact, foreign officials often complain that the Americans have too huge an agenda and want too many things from their host government. Foreign Service officers say that has become a reality of modern diplomacy.

"It's true that the U.S. government comes to them with all sorts of things," said Wechsel, who most recently served in Afghanistan. "But many foreign governments have learned to filter through all that—they know that a certain issue is really important if it's raised by the ambassador or a higher-level visitor from Washington."

Kristie Kenney

'We Come in All Shapes and Sizes'

Kristie Kenney often seems upbeat and chipper, but on the day I first met her in 2012 in Bangkok, where she was the U.S. ambassador, she was especially excited, in anticipation of a rare event the next day.

The Boeing Company was flying in its newest commercial plane, the Boeing 787 Dreamliner, which she saw as an opportunity to promote the U.S. aircraft industry, and American business in general. An added bonus was the fact that the president of Boeing for Southeast Asia who also flew in for the event, Ralph Boyce, was one of Kenney's predecessors at the embassy in Bangkok, whom many Thais still remembered because of his superb command of their language.

An event with the U.S. ambassador in almost any country would attract media attention, and Kenney used the chance to showcase issues she deemed important to American interests. Promoting U.S. business and expanding trade was one of the top issues on her agenda. "Every single day of the year we promote American companies and help to find new opportunities for Americans to do business here," she said. "It

Photo by U.S. Mission Thailand

starts with me wearing a Coca Cola T-shirt at a basketball game or carrying a Starbucks cup."

Not long after the Boeing event, Kenney gave a speech at Cotton Day, organized by Cotton USA to promote American cotton exports. She wore a dress made entirely of U.S. cotton.

Diplomatic success is often difficult to measure—many results are long-term, and the absence of conflict is rarely seen as a victory or a reason to reward someone. If there is one area where the results are as obvious and immediate as they get, it's economic and business diplomacy. Helping U.S. companies to compete on a level playing field and generate more revenue abroad, so they can contribute more to prosperity at home, is always a priority. The challenge is to ensure that those efforts truly benefit the United States and the American people, rather than just serve corporate interests and enrich powerful private businesses.

Along with her routine ambassadorial duties in Thailand, Kenney had her share of crises—both political and natural. In 2014, she had to deal with a military coup, following months of unrest. In 2011, devastating floods almost paralyzed the country, and Kenney quickly requested permission from Washington to help the Thais recover from the disaster. "We put together a flood relief package in literally 24 hours," she recalled. "I even got on the phone with Marine commanders in Okinawa, U.S. Pacific Command, and our commercial guys."

Having arrived in Bangkok soon after the 2010 WikiLeaks release of more than 250,000 diplomatic cables, some of which were secret, Kenney was concerned about the impact the public airing of private communications involving Thailand would have on her embassy's ability to do its job. Some of the post's sources "felt betrayed" when they read the cables, she said, but the "good news" is that many "still want to be engaged" with the United States. "Although there are certain people who will be more reticent with us, in general, they are interested in America and want to deal with us, so they are not going to shut us off," she added.

Kenney joined the Foreign Service in 1980 and has also been ambassador to the Philippines and Ecuador. She returned from Bangkok in 2014, and in 2016 became the counselor of the State Department, a position equal to undersecretary that provides strategic guidance to the secretary of state. She has witnessed significant changes in the conduct of U.S. diplomacy over the years. One of the them is the growing number of government agencies besides the State Department represented at embassies and consulates—and the increased numbers of their people serving there. In fact, an embassy today often resembles a mini-government.

Embassy Bangkok is one of the biggest, with about 40 agencies working on both the bilateral U.S.-Thai relationship and broader regional issues, Kenney said. There are more than 600 people focusing on global health issues, Kenney said, including employees of the Department of Health and Human Services and the Centers for Disease Control and Prevention, as well as Armed Forces medical personnel, who run a mosquito lab. According to the State Department, the United States works "to strengthen public health systems in more than 50 countries," and U.S. "health investments are at work" in almost 80 countries.

Because of the large number of people from various agencies in Bangkok attending the weekly meetings of the so-called country team, which consists of the embassy's leadership and heads of sections, some members weren't familiar with their colleagues' work. Kenney said she was "dogmatic" about not using acronyms in the meetings. "You all work for the same government," she said. "You can't give me a sentence that includes acronyms and make the rest of the room think they have no idea what you are talking about."

When Kenney decided on a diplomatic career after graduate school, her family wasn't the most understanding and wondered why she wanted to live far away from them. "My mother was furious and stopped talking to me for a couple of months," Kenney recalled. "She didn't want me living overseas. But then I ended up marrying a colleague, and she came around."

The life of Foreign Service spouses has long been more difficult than that of officers—they often have to sacrifice their own careers. To solve that problem, some spouses also join the service, only to discover that it's not that easy for "tandem couples" to secure jobs at the same post.

Photo by U.S. Mission Thailand

When Kenney was in Thailand, her husband, William Brownfield, was assistant secretary of state for international narcotics and law enforcement affairs in Washington. "When he was in Venezuela, I was in Ecuador for half of his tour and Manila for the other half," Kenney said. The more senior you get in the service, the more difficult it gets to stay together, she said. Kenney and Brownfield did serve together in several countries, including Argentina and Switzerland, earlier in their careers, and "spent a lot of time in Washington."

Another major change Kenney has witnessed in the Foreign Service is the much wider variety of duties and responsibilities officers have today—a consequence of the deep U.S. engagement across the world. The State Department's focus on having a more diverse diplomatic service in terms of ethnicity and professional background is fitting, she said, though it still has a long way to go. "We come in all shapes and sizes," she added.

As ambassador, Kenney said she strived for "good moral, a happy workforce and treating people right" at her embassies. It wasn't always easy, and she acknowledged having challenges, including one with a first-tour officer at a previous post. "She needed more coaching and mentoring, and we provided that," Kenney said. "Her immediate boss brought it to me very quickly, and we gave her every opportunity to learn and get extra help. But in the end, it wasn't enough. We all recognized it wasn't a great fit. It was entry level, so the system took care of it—she didn't get tenured and had to leave the service." Officers must qualify for tenure within five years of joining the Foreign Service or resign.

"Living overseas can be different from what people expect, or they may not be doing what they thought they would do at work, or perhaps their families are unhappy," Kenney said. "Things happen."

Ken Kero-Mentz

Fighting for Change in the Face of Prejudice

Ken Kero was working in the political section of the U.S. Embassy in Berlin in 2006, when he met a German film editor and photographer named David Mentz. Two years later, they got married and changed both their last names to Kero-Mentz.

At the time, the meaning of "married" was tricky. Germany recognized same-sex marriage "in all but name," in Ken's words, but the U.S. government, his employer, didn't acknowledge such relationships at all. In the State Department's eyes, he was single.

That was tolerable in Germany, but it became a serious difficulty when it was time for the couple to move to Ken's next post in Sri Lanka. David didn't get any of the benefits that straight Foreign Service spouses enjoyed, such as health insurance, assistance in case of emergency or evacuation and a diplomatic passport—in fact, he was ineligible for a U.S. passport of any kind.

Photo by David Kero-Mentz

What made things worse was that in Sri Lanka homosexuality was —and still is—illegal. Although the law is not enforced most of the time, for legal purposes, same-sex relationships don't exist. So for the Sri Lankan government, David had no reason to reside in the country and was only eligible for a short-term tourist visa, which had to be renewed frequently—at a Sri Lankan embassy or consulate abroad, forcing otherwise unnecessary trips. "We were traveling in and out of the country, and the fact that the government was being so difficult made it even harder for us to like the place," Ken said.

At the beginning, the American Embassy wasn't very helpful, either, he said. At least David wasn't barred from living with Ken. As for access to the embassy, the State Department left that to the discretion of every post's management, although unmarried partners—gay or straight—as well as live-in parents and other relatives, were considered "members of household."

David had access to the compound and "the ambassador treated him very well," Ken said. But the security office told the couple that, if something were to happen to David, the embassy would do nothing to help him, "because he wasn't an American and didn't have a U.S. diplomatic passport." About seven months after their arrival in Colombo, the Sri Lankan capital, a job opened up at the embassy store, and David got it— that eventually led to a longer-term visa for him.

But it was too late. The problems and the impossibility of having a more meaningful job made David "deeply unhappy," which strained their relationship, Ken said. David even contemplated going back to Germany, but in the end, he decided to stay with his husband. However, Ken cut what was supposed to be a three-year tour in Sri Lanka short, and they moved to Washington after two years.

When Hillary Clinton became secretary of state in 2009, she issued an order granting diplomatic passports, access to medical care and other benefits to employees' same-sex partners, but only those who were U.S. citizens. Foreign-born partners didn't become eligible for permanent residency and eventual citizenship until the Supreme Court's landmark 2013 overturn of the so-called Defense of Marriage Act.

David became an American citizen in 2016. Ken helped him celebrate during home leave from his tour as the political and economic section chief at the U.S. Consulate-General in Erbil, the capital of the Iraqi Kurdistan region. Family members aren't allowed in Iraq, even though Erbil is considered an oasis of stability compared to the rest of the country, so David didn't move there with Ken. This is Ken's second tour in Iraq—he was one of the first Foreign Service officers to serve in Baghdad after the 2003 overthrow of Saddam Hussein.

"It's incredibly intense, and nothing can be left until tomorrow. There is very little downtime, but despite the challenges, it's my most rewarding job in the Foreign Service to date," said Ken, who joined the service in 2000 and has also served in Brazil. Previously, he worked on Capitol Hill in Washington for five years.

The United States is trying to help Iraq through a precarious security situation, including a grave threat from the self-proclaimed Islamic State, coupled with an acrimonious political environment and a struggling economy. Erbil's proximity to IS territory in the north magnifies its importance.

While serving in Washington between his tours in Sri Lanka and Iraq, Ken got to work on issues that affected his and David's life, as well as the lives of millions of gay, lesbian, bisexual and transgender people around the world. He was president of GLIFAA, an organization of LGBT employees of the State Department and other foreign affairs agencies. It was founded in 1992—until then, diplomats who were found out or admitted to being gay were often expelled from the Foreign Service.

GLIFAA's initial priority was to secure full equality for American LGBT employees and their families. Several years ago, transgender rights were added to its agenda, which has since expanded even further to include non-American LGBT staff members of U.S. embassies, consulates and other diplomatic missions abroad, particularly those in countries where being gay is still illegal or dangerous.

After the brutal 2016 murder of Xulhaz Mannan, a 39-year-old employee of the embassy in Bangladesh and editor of the country's first

David Kero-Mentz (left), Ken's husband, became a U.S. citizen in 2016.
Photo by Tiffany Marlowe

and only LGBT magazine, "we are putting even more of an emphasis on the needs of our local staff," Kero-Mentz said. In fact, GLIFAA has tried to help the global fight for LGBT rights, partly by "developing the framework" that led to the creation of a special envoy position at the State Department last year, he added. Secretary of State John Kerry made a point of entrusting an openly gay Foreign Service officer, Randy Berry, with that job.

"That is a lasting legacy and demonstrates the crossover work of GLIFAA," Kero-Mentz said. "It's not just about working to resolve personnel issues, but also to improve the work of the State Department on LGBT issues globally."

One personnel matter that is still unresolved is the diplomatic accreditation of same-sex Foreign Service families to countries where marriage equality or even domestic partnerships don't exist, Kero-Mentz said. That effectively precludes LGBT diplomats from serving in much of the world.

Despite all the challenges over the years, as well as the dangers of living in certain places and being away from home, Kero-Mentz said he has appreciated the opportunities for public service and "enjoyed experiencing things few Americans have experienced." He advised new diplomats to focus on the big picture.

"Roll with the punches, don't let the small stuff wear you down, and take even difficult experiences as opportunities to learn something new, whether it's substantive or interpersonal," he said.

Tracey Jacobson

The Luxury of
an Ambassador's Autonomy

Tracey Jacobson had been in Turkmenistan for about six hours as
the new, 38-year-old American ambassador to the former Soviet republic in 2003, when she went to present her credentials to President
Saparmurat Niyazov.

Along with the traditional pleasantries, however, Jacobson warned
the 63-year-old leader that his country risked U.S. sanctions under the
International Freedom of Religion Act. "According to the Turkmen law
at the time, you had to have at least 500 registered members of your religious organization to be legal," said Jacobson, a Foreign Service officer since 1988. "In practice, that meant only state-controlled Islam and
the Russian Orthodox Church were legal, and any others were illegal
and subject to sometimes quite brutal harassment. Even the Catholics
weren't registered."

Photo by U.S. Mission Kosovo

The ambassador told Niyazov, who died in 2006, that she wanted to "work with his government to avoid these sanctions. Within six months, they changed the law to require only five members in order to register a religious group," she recalled. "I'm not saying religion became completely free, but it became significantly better."

U.S. ambassadors often complain that they have lost much of the autonomy they used to enjoy in the last century, before modern technology, instant communication and easy travel made it possible for officials in Washington to look over their shoulders from thousands of miles away. That is particularly true for ambassadors to countries that command constant White House attention, such as Russia and China.

In smaller or less challenging countries, however, the direction set by Washington is often so broad that an ambassador's hand is much freer in shaping U.S. diplomacy. The change in the Turkmen law "wasn't the result of discussions back in Washington," Jacobson said. "It was the result of drinking a lot of coffee in my living room and talking about what we should do."

Another embassy achievement—in Tajikistan, another former Soviet republic, where Jacobson became ambassador in 2006—was not directed by Washington, either. When she first arrived, there was no American Chamber of Commerce in the country, so she tasked her economic section with mobilizing the business community to establish a chamber. "You want business people coming together and lobbying the government to create the best business environment," she said. "We started by using the embassy's convening authority to set up business forums. Some of the business leaders told us that they had never talked to each other until we brought them together."

In the absence of a dedicated commercial section, officers and contractors from the U.S. Agency for International Development stepped in to help "improve the business environment, reduce the bureaucracy, and make it easier to start and grow a business," Jacobson said. "We had advisors working with various ministries, and we also did entrepreneur training."

Even today, some of the authorities of an ambassador are quite meaningful, she added—for example, a new position cannot be created and a new employee cannot be sent to post without the ambassador's approval. While in Tajikistan, Jacobson said she refused an initial request from Washington to add positions at her embassy, because there were not enough management officers to take care of the post's personnel. "I made a decision that we would not allow the American staff to increase until our management platform was appropriate for the mission," she said. "I went on a lobbying campaign, which was ultimately effective. Then I was able to accept additional positions."

Jacobson attributed that particular success largely to the knowledge and experience she had gained as a management officer in the Foreign

Service. Officers with management and administration as a career track —or "cone"—are sometimes looked down on by their colleagues for not being "real diplomats," because they don't deal with foreign policy.

But Jacobson, who has also been ambassador to Kosovo, defended management as an "honorable cone" and said she was "proud" to be a management officer. "As a management officer, you negotiate leases, telecommunications, customs and shipping, or you work with the Foreign Ministry trying to get a school recognized," she said. "If you are chief of mission and only care about policy and politics, you will probably be less effective, because your team will not be working to its maximum capacity," she said.

Having earned a master's degree in Soviet studies and international economics from Johns Hopkins University, Jacobson learned and honed her management skills during her first tours in the Foreign Service—in South Korea, Russia and the Bahamas. She then became deputy executive secretary at the National Security Council, which added interagency policy facilitation to her skill set.

Even so, when Jacobson sought to become deputy chief of mission in Latvia, yet another former Soviet republic, she faced opposition because of her career track—the powers that be preferred someone in the political cone. "There was a lot of trepidation, but it worked out," she said. Within a week of her arrival in Riga, the ambassador felt comfortable enough to go on leave for six weeks, she added. Later during her tour, the embassy received a "very good inspection report" from the State Department's Office of the Inspector-General, "and that's how I came to the attention of people in Washington as a potential ambassador."

Photo by U.S. Mission Kosovo

Between overseas tours, Jacobson has dedicated some of her career to training and professional development of the Foreign Service. She was deputy director of the Foreign Service Institute for two years, beginning in 2010, and the following year chaired a promotion panel—the service's promotion system has received more complaints from career diplomats during my research than any other issue.

Jacobson has read hundreds of evaluation reports. "The one comment that stuck in my mind was, 'There are many stars in the Foreign Service, but this one is a supernova.' What does that mean? Are they about to collapse into a black hole? But that's not the norm" in performance reviews, Jacobson said. It's true, however, that "success has many fathers, and sometimes several people claim credit for the same thing, because policy successes require a team effort," she added.

Performance reviews are supposed to be written each year by an officer's immediate supervisor, with the officer's input. In the late 1990s and early 2000s, many reports were said to have been written—or at least drafted—by the employee, but that has changed, Jacobson said. A more likely scenario today, she said, is for the boss to ask the employee for a list of his or her accomplishments and write the review, on which the officer has the right to comment in a dedicated section, and even to disagree with the content.

"You should own your evaluation," Jacobson said. "You should provide your boss with robust input, read it and sign it. You are also supposed to have documented counseling throughout the year. When it comes time for me to write your evaluation, I can't remember everything, but if we have sessions and write down what's going on, it's much easier. People used to just make up counseling dates. These days, people take this more seriously."

Steve Kashkett

'You Don't Have to Be a Senior Officer to Do Cool Things'

When Steve Kashkett became the U.S. consul-general in Halifax, Nova Scotia, in 2001, he was fully aware that his new position would not help his career. There was only one reason for his decision: He wanted to be close to Baltimore, his American home, so he could see his children and "maintain joint custody," following his recent divorce.

"For three years, I flew to Baltimore almost every other weekend," Kashkett recalled. "Divorce and child custody are difficult in any marriage, but it's 10 times more difficult in the Foreign Service. How do you maintain joint custody if you are assigned on the other side of the world? You have to devise a much more complex set of arrangements."

Photo by U.S. Department of State

Many of Kashkett's colleagues in a similar position, as well as those with elderly parents, "gravitate to Canada and Mexico," he said. In addition to its embassies in Ottawa and Mexico City, the United States has seven consulates in Canada and nine in Mexico. Canada is certainly quieter than Mexico, though his job in Halifax was still important, Kashkett said—"there is more trade between Canada's four eastern provinces, which our consulate in Halifax covers, and the U.S. than we have with most countries."

Kashkett has served in Mexico, too. As consul-general in Tijuana from 2009 until 2012, he worked with the local authorities to "help them deal with drug-cartel violence 10 miles from downtown San Diego—bodies hanging from bridges, gun battles in the streets—so it didn't spill over on our side of the border."

During his more than three decades in the Foreign Service, Kashkett has been posted to both relatively tranquil places, such as Prague, where he was deputy chief of mission from 2013 until 2016, and difficult spots like Haiti and the Palestinian territories earlier in his career. Paris is typically considered a plush post, but France has long been a terrorist target. Since 1970, more than 400 people have been killed and over 1,700 wounded in dozens of attacks. The deadliest were the coordinated Islamic State attacks in November 2015.

Kashkett served as a counter-terrorism officer at the embassy in Paris during the 1980s, the decade with more attacks than any other—over 30—although the 2010s are quickly catching up. He helped build the case for the conviction of Georges Ibrahim Abdallah, a Lebanese militant who was sentenced to life in prison for the 1982 murder of a U.S. assistant military attache and an Israeli diplomat. The 1987 trial attracted so much media and public attention that Kashkett, having been a "visible presence" in the prosecution's case, became "the first American diplomat to be evacuated from Paris for security reasons since World War II," he said.

He also faced security challenges in the early 1990s as a political officer in Jerusalem, where part of his job was to "visit every Israeli settlement in the West Bank to get a gauge of how much expansion was going on— settlements were seen as one of the main obstacles to peace negotiations," he said. However, those challenges paled to the security restrictions his colleagues have to deal with today, he added.

Even though the first Palestinian intifada was still going on, "it was a period of great hope and possibility" that a peace agreement might be within reach, Kashkett said. "We were able to go out in the West Bank by ourselves, without a security escort. Today, no one can do that. It affects your ability to find out what's going on and talk to ordinary people. If you go to meet a Palestinian activist in a three-vehicle security convoy, you'd have a very different interaction than if you met discreetly in a cafe. So the heavy security we have in many countries today affects the way we conduct diplomacy," he said.

Kashkett holds the rank of minister counselor, the Foreign Service equivalent to a two-star general. But he said some of his most interesting and rewarding experiences happened while he was a junior and mid-level officer. "You don't have to be a senior officer to do cool things," he said. One of his assignments in the late 1980s was to "develop a relationship with a radical Haitian Roman Catholic priest" named Jean-Bertrand Aristide. Among the main activities of U.S. embassies is identifying promising figures with potential for leadership in their respective countries, and engaging with them early on in their careers. Kashkett's bosses at the time saw such potential in Aristide, who became Haiti's first democratically elected president in 1991 at the age of 38.

After just seven months in office, Aristide was deposed in a military coup but was restored with U.S. help in 1994 and served out the remaining two years of his term. He returned as president in 2001, only to be ousted in another coup in 2004, in which he accused the United States of being involved. Washington denied that, although it had criticized his governing style.

In addition to his overseas assignments, Kashkett has served in various positions in Washington, including as vice president of the American Foreign Service Association (AFSA), the union of U.S. diplomats, during President George W. Bush's second term. In 2007, following a

Steve Kashkett and his wife, Wendy Goldman, in Prague.
Photo by U.S. Mission Czech Republic

town hall meeting at the State Department where a few employees objected to Secretary of State Condoleezza Rice's intention to force career diplomats to serve in Iraq, the Foreign Service was viewed by many as disobedient and disloyal. "There was a false perception that we were spoiled brats," Kashkett said.

AFSA worked tirelessly with the department's leadership to avoid "directed assignments," which had not been used since the Vietnam War. But the administration needed thousands of diplomats to staff what became the largest embassy in the world, as well as several so-called provincial reconstruction teams throughout Iraq, so "we were under enormous pressure," Kashkett said. "Directed assignments would have fundamentally changed our service. We rose to the task and managed the staffing through volunteer bidding. We negotiated a series of incentives and motivated enough people to volunteer."

AFSA also opposed the management's attempt to give outsized weight to service in war zones in determining who got promoted. "Some people can't go to war zones because they are single parents, but they still do great work elsewhere" Kashkett said.

Family considerations often add challenges to an already difficult Foreign Service career, and they derailed Kashkett's most recent posting. After returning from Prague in the summer of 2016, he was supposed to go to the embassy in Australia as political counselor. But medical and family-related issues made such a faraway assignment very difficult.

"So I reluctantly broke that assignment, which is a very precarious position to be in at this stage in late summer, but someone is about to get a message that my job is available and will be very happy," Kashkett said. "Something else will come up for me. The Foreign Service ethic is all about flexibility and resilience."

Index

Made in the USA
Monee, IL
14 October 2022

15855251R00045